S_{elect} A_n I_{deal} L_{ife}

Your 59-Minute Guide to Enjoying the Journey of Life

By Jordan I. Maness, M.Ed.

INTRODUCTION

Do you want to be happier? Would you like to reduce your stress and increase your joy and fulfillment? Modern research indicates that happy people tend to earn more money, live longer, and have better relationships. Or as Shawn Achor, the author of 'The Happiness Advantage,' says: "Happiness fuels success, not the other way around." But have you noticed that everyone seems to have different advice about how to be happier? With thousands of books, videos, seminars, retreats, motivational podcasts, and self-help gurus and guides providing lengthy and sometimes conflicting instructions on finding greater fulfillment, it's easy to feel overwhelmed and confused. Where should you begin? What is Step 1?

Finally there's a solution. It's quite literally in your hands. This short booklet will serve as your starting point to understanding the fundamentals of being happy. As a certified life coach with an unquenchable and authentic curiosity regarding the subject matter and with over a decade of experience working as a career counselor at UCLA, I've researched the top self-development books, resources, and philosophies out there and discovered that there were many common themes among them. Whether the messages came from writings hundreds of years old or 21st century TED Talks, the central themes kept repeating themselves. I've condensed these core messages into one quick and memorable analogy that will help you identify the areas in your life in most need of improvement. This is an interactive book for people who are ready to take action to improve their life but are short on time and need to know where to begin. After reading this booklet, you can more confidently and effectively choose additional resources that will address the key areas in your life that are affecting your level of happiness. The following memorable analogy will serve as your guide to experiencing more joy, fulfillment, and hope in your life. These positive emotions make up an overall state of deep happiness. This is an inner state of peace and well being that isn't controlled by external conditions. It's a feeling of flow, confidence, and harmony with the world that sustains, even while experiencing a whole spectrum of other emotions. This type of happiness comes when you follow the principles in this booklet. And when you do, your happiness will contribute to the betterment of the world. That's a win-win. Scottish novelist Robert Louis Stevenson said, **"There is no duty we so much underrate as the duty of being happy. By being happy, we sow anonymous benefits upon the world."**

Are you ready to fulfill the duty of being happy? Why or why not?

_____

_____

_____

_____

_____

_____

_____

_____

_____

_____

_____

_____

_____

THE SAILBOAT

By now you have probably realized that the acronym for "Select An Ideal Life" is S.A.I.L. That's no coincidence. The word "sail" means to move along easily and gracefully. Now that sounds like an appealing way to maneuver through life! We all have the potential to sail through life with more joy and less resistance, but we need perspective and helpful tools to utilize on the journey. Are you interested? Are you ready to S.A.I.L.?

On a sailboat as in life, our path is rarely a straight line, and the adventure of being out at sea is often equally or even more fulfilling than reaching the destination. When we reach the end of life, we won't be patting ourselves on our backs for how quickly we made it to the end of our lives but rather for the quality of our experiences and the manner in which we conducted ourselves on our journey through life. American author Ursula K. Le Guin said, **"It is good to have an end to journey toward; but it is the journey that matters, in the end."** American author Margaret Lee Runbeck said, **"Happiness is not a state to arrive at, but a manner of traveling."**

When you are out at sea, each day has the potential to be exciting and enjoyable no matter where you are. Your life will have all kinds of twists and turns and much like a sailboat out on the open seas, you can set course in whatever direction you desire. You'll steer your vessel to the best of your ability but the winds may push you in an unintended direction. Sometimes you'll let go and enjoy where the wind takes you and sometimes you will make the necessary adjustments to route yourself back towards the specific destinations you had in-mind. No two life paths will be identical.

When you begin to implement and reflect on the perspectives and strategies presented in this guide, you'll find yourself beginning to sail, beginning to experience life as a more magnificent journey. American professional tennis player Arthur Ashe said, **"Success is a journey, not a destination. The doing is often more important than the outcome."** A Chinese Proverb states, **"The journey is the reward."**

Are you racing through life? If so, how? If not, what are you doing to enjoy the journey? What do you do to ensure that you experience some fulfillment each day? What can you do to experience more joy throughout the journey?

_____

_____

_____

_____

_____

_____

_____

_____

_____

_____

_____

_____

_____

_____

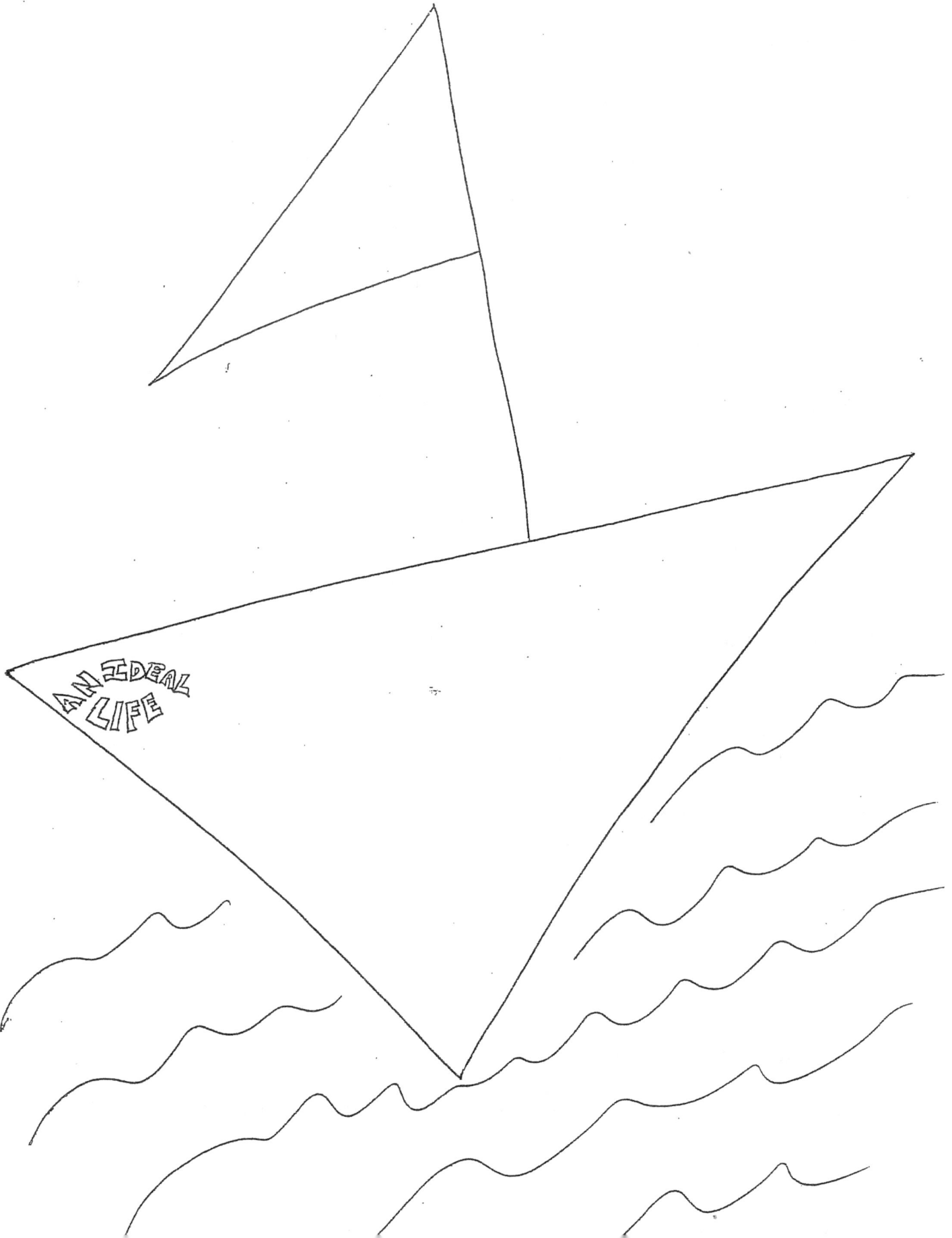

AN IDEAL LIFE

THE NAME OF YOUR BOAT

Have you ever walked around a marina and noticed the names on the back of all the boats? Well your boat has a name too, and it describes the type of life you will choose to live. Your boat is called, "An Ideal Life." What I mean by "Ideal" is two-fold. First of all, ideal is defined as wonderful, perfect, and dreamy. Thinking about, assessing, and discovering the type of life that captivates your attention, utilizes your talents, and generates deep fulfillment for you is a critical step. Believing you deserve this fantastic life and choosing to create that for yourself, is equally important. As Italian artist Michelangelo said, **"The greater danger for most of us lies not in setting our aim too high and falling short; but in setting our aim too low, and achieving our mark."**

But the real secret to creating the "ideal" is to adopt the attitude of "I-deal". The way you deal with the external circumstances of your life directly and profoundly affects your level of happiness. You have a choice every moment of every day and that is to select your attitude and your response to the experiences of your life. Holocaust survivor Viktor Frankl stated, **"The one thing you can't take away from me is the way I choose to respond to what you do to me. The last of one's freedoms is to choose one's attitude**

in any given circumstance." Sonya Lyubomirsky, author of "The How of Happiness" states that 50% of your happiness is determined by a genetically determined "happiness set-point." The 50% you control is composed of your life circumstances (10%) and by how you think and behave (40%). The reason only 10% of your happiness is affected by your life circumstances is due to a powerful phenomenon termed 'hedonic adaptation.' In other words, something that at first gives you a big boost in happiness, soon becomes your new normal and you endlessly desire more. Thus, focusing on putting in the work and developing positive habits of thought and action is critical and much more influential for sustaining your levels of happiness. Ingraining new and improved habits is a skill that can be developed and with practice and modern science has shown that you can re-wire your brain and thus change automatic thought patterns. As you develop healthy and empowering habitual thoughts, actions and reactions, your level of happiness will rise, and over time, your life will begin to profoundly transform.

By creating proactive systems and choosing healthy responses to the events of your life you'll be well on your way to living your ideal life. Roman emperor Marcus Aurelius said, **"Very little is needed to make a happy life; it is all within yourself, in your way of thinking."**

Selecting An "I-deal" Life leads to an "ideal" life. Legendary college basketball coach John Wooden said, **"Things turn out best for those who make the best of the way things turn out."** Polish-American pianist Arthur Rubinstein stated, **"Love life and life will love you back."**

Describe in detail your ideal vision for your life. Do you believe you deserve the life you've described? Why or why not? Do you have an I-deal attitude? Why or why not?

_____

_____

_____

_____

_____

_____

_____

_____

_____

_____

_____

_____

_____

_____

AN IDEAL LIFE

THE CAPTAIN

What is both a magnificent gift and an enormous responsibility is the fact that you are the "captain" of this boat. You are ultimately in-charge of your own life. The direction in which you set sail and what you do with all that comes your way along your journey is in your hands.

American author and teacher Bob Moawad said, **"The best day of your life is the one in which you decide your life is your own. No apologies or excuses. No one to lean on, rely on, or blame. The gift is yours-it is an amazing journey-and you alone are responsible for the quality of it. This is the day our life really begins."** In her book, "The Top 5 Regrets of the Dying," former palliative care nurse Bronnie Ware reveals that the most common regret she heard from people who were in the last few weeks of their lives was: "I wish I had the courage to live a life true to myself, not the life others expected of me." Don't let your life slip by without realizing the importance of being captain of your own life.

Have faith that you are more than capable of wearing the captain's hat. As American poet and essayist Ralph Waldo Emerson said, **"What lies behind us and what lies before us are tiny matters compared to what lies within us."** You are capable of doing things beyond your imagination, but this requires the courage to put on the captain's hat in order to find out. American inventor and scientist Thomas Edison said, **"If we all did the things we are capable of doing, we would literally astound ourselves."** So put on the captain's hat and declare that you are taking responsibility and ownership for your life.

Do you feel you are capable of successfully taking charge of your own life? Why or why not? In what areas of your life are you living up to your potential? In which areas could you take more accountability for your actions?

_____

_____

_____

_____

_____

_____

_____

_____

_____

_____

_____

_____

AN IDEAL LIFE

THE LIFE JACKET

As captain out at sea, it's important to wear your "life jacket." Your life jacket is your protection from mistakes. Your protection comes from your attitude and belief about the value of making mistakes and it will help you overcome your fear of making them. You will experience mishaps and every decision you make won't be perfect. Mistakes don't have to drown you; they can actually propel you forward depending on how you look at them. American poet and essayist Ralph Waldo Emerson said, **"Our greatest glory is not in never failing but in rising up every time we fail."** Inventor and scientist Thomas Edison said, **"I have not failed, I've just found 10,000 ways that won't work."**

You cannot fail as long as you remember that failure is simply not learning from a mistake. Irish writer and poet James Joyce said, **"A man's errors are his portals of discovery."** Continuously looking for the lessons in your experiences will keep you afloat. Remember, this approach is your life jacket. As you enthusiastically find and apply the lessons that have come from your mistakes, you'll continue to enhance your belief in yourself and at the same time, you'll begin to feel more optimistic about the future. Cultivating this optimism is important. Research has shown that optimists have better psychological and physical health. A recent study at the University of Illinois revealed that optimists may be twice as likely to be in perfect heart health than pessimistic individuals. According to the Mayo Clinic, optimists have stronger immune systems and lower rates of depression.

Remember, you jeopardize reaching unchartered levels of happiness if you are afraid of making a mistake. As Anglo-American poet and playwright TS Eliot said, **"Only those that risk going too far can possibly find out how far they can go."** French author Andre Gide said, **"Man cannot discover new oceans unless he has the courage to lose sight of the shore."** So take action, put on your life jacket, and declare, "I am not afraid to make mistakes, for whatever happens, I will take the lesson and become stronger and more enlightened because of it."

Have you adopted the "I'm okay with making mistakes" mind-set? Where in your life do you have a fear of failure that's preventing you from reaching your goals? What lessons have you learned from your past mistakes? What would you do if you weren't afraid of failing?

_____

_____

_____

_____

_____

_____

_____

_____

_____

_____

_____

_____

_____

_____

THE COMPASS

On the journey of life, there likely will be times when you aren't sure which way to steer or if you are taking steps in a direction that makes sense for you. But like all great sailboat captains, you'll carry a trusty "compass" to help guide you. Your compass is your gut-instinct. As you look at the path you are on and the decisions you are making, you can check-in to see if they are in-tune with what your instincts are telling you. If so, you'll feel much more confident that your choices will be successful.

The more frequently we tune-in to the inner-wisdom of our gut-instinct, the clearer the communication channel becomes. Our instincts are seldom wrong and often they provide something of a "sixth sense" for us to rely upon. Most of us can point to times we made a decision but just didn't feel good about it for some reason. That "reason" was probably our instincts telling us we were on the wrong path. Or perhaps, you've had the opposite experience where you felt very confident about a particular decision even though you didn't necessarily have a strong logical case for making that decision. You were probably quite in-tune with your gut-instinct at the time. American poet and essayist, Ralph Waldo Emerson said, **"Trust your instinct to the end, though you can render no reason."** American pediatrician and author,

Benjamin Spock declared, **"Trust yourself. You know more than you think."**

Sometimes there is a great deal of "noise" in our heads that we need to silence in-order to hear our inner wisdom. Meditation and breathwork can be a very helpful tool to utilize to help create these optimal conditions for us to connect with our compass. Research on the effects of meditation has shown that a regular practice can reduce anxiety, lower stress, improve concentration, and even slow the aging process of the brain. There are many different meditation techniques so find the one that works best for you. The more you do it and the more you connect with your instinct, the clearer your decisions will become and the more you will be able to rely on your compass.

Are you in-tune with your gut-instinct, and do you trust it? Sit in a quiet room, close your eyes, and take a series of long, slow, deep breaths. Ask yourself what one thing in life should you start or stop doing to be a better version of yourself? Listen to what answer instinctively comes to you and write it down here.

_____

_____

_____

_____

_____

_____

_____

_____

_____

_____

_____

THE JOURNAL

Just like many adventurers of the past, you too will keep a special journal. As you are living out your life's journey, one of the most important tools you can utilize to enhance your level of happiness is to keep a daily gratitude journal. American author and speaker Tony Robbins said, **"When you are grateful, fear disappears and abundance appears."** UC-Davis Professor of Psychology Robert A. Emmons has said that practicing gratitude can lower blood pressure, improve immune function, facilitate more efficient sleep while also reducing lifetime risk for depression and anxiety.

When "out at sea", notice all the good that you have in your life, from the smallest blessing to the largest, and be sure to let the positive moments and experiences sink in. American publisher and author William Feather said, **"Plenty of people miss their share of happiness, not because they never found it, but because they didn't stop to enjoy it."** Pay attention to your good fortunes. The more you start to do this, the easier it is to do because you'll be training your mind to hone in on the good things happening around you instead of all the negatives. French novelist Colette said, **"What a wonderful life I've had. I only wish I'd realized it sooner."** Greek philosopher Epictetus said, **"He is a wise man who does not grieve for the**

things which he has not, but rejoices for those which he has." Be grateful for your strengths, talents, and gifts.

It will take self-discipline to make entries into your gratitude journal daily but eventually it will be a part of your day that you truly look forward to. These entries can be in writing or drawings or photos or the like. This journal will help you deepen the joy you already have in your life and will help you keep your attention on attracting more happiness and fulfillment into your life. Obtain a blank journal and start making entries of gratitude today.

List 10 things you are grateful for and why:

1.

_____

2.

_____

3.

_____

4.

_____

5.

_____

6.

_____

7.

_____

8.

_____

9.

_____

10.

_____

THE COOLER

Your "cooler" is how you fuel your physical and overall well-being. Eating healthy, exercising and taking care of your body to the best of your ability is a very important part of your ideal life. Keep in-mind that exercise is beneficial in more ways than just your physical health. John Ratay, Author and Associate Professor at Harvard Medical School, states that "exercise helps optimize our brain's ability to learn, helps us regulate our emotions, and increases motivation."

It takes energy to continue on your journey with enthusiasm and packing your cooler with healthy food and lots of drinking water is a great starting place. Of course, getting proper rest and developing a healthy way of managing stress are also both critical. Pay attention to how certain foods make you feel and consult with health experts to find a diet and exercise plan that meets your body's needs. Find a healthy way to deal with stress-perhaps through journaling, exercising, talking to a close friend, meditating or something else that works for you. By developing daily rituals and habits that support your health, you'll optimize the chances of sustaining your vitality.

By doing all of the above, you'll be providing yourself with the foundation required to build your ideal life. It's a lot easier to have an "I-deal" approach when you are feeling healthy and strong. Classic Roman poet Virgil stated, **"The greatest wealth is health."** An Arabian Proverb states, **"He who has health has hope; and he who has hope has everything."**

In what ways are you taking great care of your mental and physical well-being? What daily health rituals do you have or want to have? How do you manage stress? What one new habit that would improve your health can you start today?

_____

_____

_____

_____

_____

_____

_____

_____

_____

_____

_____

_____

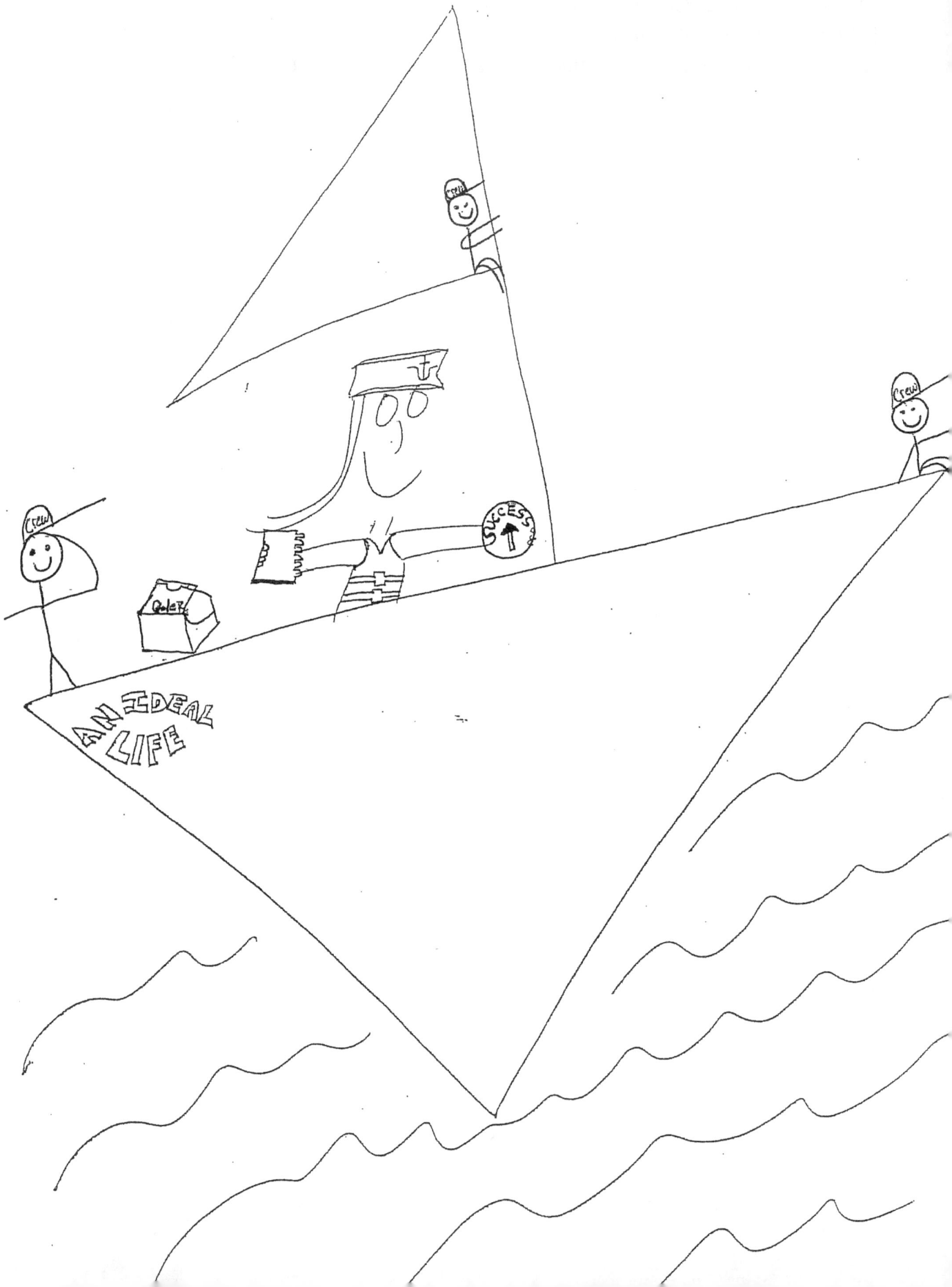

Crew

Crew

Crew

SUCCESS

AN IDEAL LIFE

THE CREW

Although you are the captain of your life's journey, to Select An Ideal Life and to find a deep sense of joy and fulfillment in life, it will be important for you to assemble a solid "crew" of supporters. Through his research, Positive Psychologist and Author, Tal Ben-Shahar has found that the number one predictor of happiness is the time we spend with people we care about and who care about us.

Who are you spending your time with? Who is there to support you when things get tough in your life? Who can you talk to about your feelings?

Taking time to build and sustain positive relationships in your life is indispensable. Close friends, family-members, teachers, mentors, counselors, colleagues, and other positive and inspiring people will help you learn about yourself, maneuver through the twists and turns of your life and regain your confidence during challenging times. French novelist Marcel Proust said, **"Let us be grateful to people who make us happy, they are the charming gardeners who make our souls blossom."** English physicist Isaac Newton said, **"If I have seen further than others, it is by standing upon the shoulders of giants."** And American television host, actress, producer, and philanthropist Oprah Winfrey said, **"No matter how diligent or persistent you have been, there is not one of us who made this journey toward**

success by ourselves." Don't be afraid to ask for help. Asking for help is one of the bravest things you can do and provides others an opportunity to feel a sense of self-worth that comes with aiding another.

As you think about your crew, take a close look at the people you spend your time with. Are they supportive, positive people who inspire you to be the best version of yourself? Or are you spending time with people who put you down and turn their back on you when things get tough? American author Mark Twain said, **"Keep away from those that try to belittle your ambitions. Small people always do that, but the really great make you believe that you too can become great."** Perhaps there are people you'd like to have as mentors or friends in your life. One of the best ways to create these ties is to help people create their own ideal lives; in essence, serve on their crew. There is a Buddhist saying: **"If you light the lamp for somebody, it will also brighten your path."**

*Who is currently on your crew? Who would you like to have on your crew?
What changes regarding your crew do you need to make and why? Whose crew
are you currently serving on?*

_____

_____

_____

_____

_____

_____

_____

_____

_____

_____

_____

_____

_____

AN IDEAL LIFE

Crew

Crew

Crew

Color

SUCCESS

THE SAILS

As you create your ideal life, you'll need to develop your top strengths and life skills to help you move along your journey more effectively. These skills are your "sails". Life skills are competencies such as time-management, effective communication, goal-setting, budgeting, organization, decision-making, problem-solving, and flexibility. They will assist you to maneuver through life more easily and can be built through taking classes, seminars, workshops, and through daily practice. Additionally, you'll want to be sure to utilize your unique strengths and talents frequently. Martin Seligman, Professor of Psychology at the University of Pennsylvania is frequently referred to as the founder of positive psychology. His research led him to define a meaningful life as one where an individual uses his/her unique strengths for a purpose greater than him/herself.

Use and enhance your top strengths and at the same time, learn new life-skills. American author and speaker Denis Waitley said, **"All the top achievers I know are life-long learners...Looking for new skills, insights, and ideas. If they're not learning, they're not growing...not moving toward excellence."**

Life is a grand classroom and these skills will constantly be tested and honed. Take them seriously and discover areas you can improve upon. Also, find ways to use your top gifts and talents frequently. American author and educator George Leonard said, **"Much of the world's depression and discontent can ultimately be traced to our unused energy – our own untapped potential."** As you use your top strengths and develop your life skills, not only will your confidence grow, but you'll find you're able to use your "sails" to much more effectively maneuver through your life.

Rank yourself from 1-10 with 10 being optimal in the following areas:

	1	2	3	4	5	6	7	8	9	10
Time Management										
Effective Communication										
Goal-setting										
Budgeting										
Organization										
Decision-making										
Problem-solving										
Flexibility										

What are your top skills (listed above or others), and how are you finding ways to frequently capitalize on them in your life? What skills do you need to develop?

_____

_____

_____

_____

_____

_____

_____

THE ANCHOR

As you move through life, there will be choppy waters. There will be periods or experiences that will be extremely challenging when you may need to "drop anchor" in order to re-group and weather the storm. These may be obstacles, setbacks, or tragedies. Although your positive mindset, self-confidence, supporters, and life-skills will help you overcome these challenges, it's also critical to have an "anchor" to rely upon.

This "anchor" is something bigger than yourself that you can count on throughout your life. This can be a cause you believe in or a power greater than yourself that you resonate with. It doesn't matter as long as it is something that is bigger than you and something you can connect with and can put energy towards regularly; especially when things in your personal or professional life are not going smoothly (but even when they are). Do not wait until an emergency to see if you have an anchor on-board. Make time for and continuously put energy towards something(s) bigger than yourself throughout your life.

Your anchor will help you more confidently move forward with your life. Your anchor will help you feel that your life has purpose and meaning. American author and speaker Denis Waitley said, **"No man or woman is an island. To exist just for yourself is meaningless. You can achieve the** most satisfaction when you feel related to some greater purpose in life, something greater than yourself." American author and activist Helen Keller echoed these sentiments, "Many persons have the wrong idea of what constitutes true happiness. It is not attained through self-gratification but through fidelity to a worthy purpose." United States President Barack Obama has also stated similar ideas, "It's only when you hitch your wagon to something larger than yourself that you realize your true potential."

What is your anchor? Is there a cause or power greater than yourself that you believe in? What are you doing to invest in that cause or power?

_____

_____

_____

_____

_____

_____

_____

_____

_____

THE STARS

"Stars" are the inspiration that lights up our world and fuels us and propels us onward in life. Without inspiration, you may feel unmotivated, apathetic, or stuck. Many adventurers in the past looked up at the stars for guidance and inspiration on their long journeys across the seas. Throughout life you'll find your own inspiration in many forms. The key is to proactively seek it regularly and capitalize on the push of momentum ignited within you.

Your stars can be anything that energizes and inspires your journey. For example, a selfless neighbor, an invigorating speaker, a soulful musician, a hard-working grocery clerk, new scientific discovery, a beautiful waterfall, a touching news-story, an extremely talented juggler, a child's drawing, a baby's laugh, or any of the every day people surrounding us who are doing amazing things and contributing to our world in incredible ways. Be present, and look up from time to time to take notice of the motivating and inspiring world we live in. You can't always wait to be inspired; sometimes you have to go seek inspiration.

Patanjali, who compiled the Yoga Sutras, stated, **"When you are inspired... your mind transcends limitations, your consciousness expands in every direction, and you find yourself in a new, great, and wonderful world."** So open your eyes to the magic and beauty that is happening all around you. Feel the inspiration and take action. Before you know it, you will become a shining star for somebody else. You will know how to Select An Ideal Life and you will be living a life beyond your dreams.

Who or what inspires you? How do you regularly seek inspiration?

_____

_____

_____

_____

_____

_____

_____

_____

_____

_____

_____

_____

_____

_____

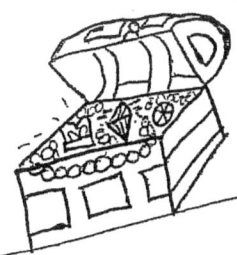

THE TREASURES

On your life's journey, there will be certain goals, experiences, titles, degrees, jobs, relationships, accomplishments, and tangible items that you desire. These are the "treasures" that help to make your life's journey that much more enriching. By following the strategies and concepts introduced thus far in this booklet, you will have laid the foundation for successfully achieving a great many of your treasures along the way.

It is essential that the goals you are setting are in-tune with your own passions and values. Get to know yourself and create a life that reflects your own definition of success. Greek philosopher Aristotle stated, **"Knowing yourself is the beginning of all wisdom."** Throughout your life's journey you will discover a great deal about yourself; especially when you try new things and meet new people. Take time to reflect on what you've learned about yourself as you have experiences in life, and construct your definition of living successfully based on what you've learned. Former Secretary General of the United Nations Kofi Annan said, **"To live is to choose. But to choose well, you must know who you are and what you stand for, where you want to go and why you want to get there."** As you are living your life and setting goals guided by your own definition of living successfully, many people will voice their opinion about the course you are on and oftentimes they will have a different definition of what it means to be living successfully. Be sure to check with your own definition for guidance. American author and journalist Anna Quindlen said, **"If your success is not on your own terms, if it looks good to the world but does not feel good in your heart, it is not success at all."**

One treasure many people want to discover is their dream job. A dream job can be defined as one that is a great fit for your interests, skills, and values. There may be several careers that are a good match for you. Be sure to get clear on your top talents, what captivates your attention, and what matters most to you in a job and then explore and pursue options that are in harmony with these factors.

If you are having difficulty figuring out what other goals you want to pursue, ask yourself what are the things that the best version of yourself wants you to start doing or stop doing. Ask yourself what makes you enjoy life and what makes you feel good about yourself. Ask yourself what experiences you'll regret if you never get the chance to try them. It's okay to pursue one goal and then change your mind and pursue another once more information is revealed about yourself or your choice. The key is to strive to make choices that are more and more aligned with who you truly are and what you truly want. Once you do obtain some of your treasures, take time to

savor and mindfully enjoy them.

What is your definition of living successfully? Are you crafting your goals based on your own definition of success? Are you passionate about achieving these goals? What small and large treasures are you seeking right now and why?

_____

_____

_____

_____

_____

_____

_____

_____

_____

_____

_____

THE TREASURE MAP

As you define and go after your goals, your treasures in life, it will be helpful to utilize a "treasure map" to assist you in reaching your goals. Once you have a goal that matters to you, go after it with passion and the path will appear. American motivational speaker Earl Nightingale stated, **"The more intensely we feel about an idea or a goal, the more assuredly the idea, buried deep in our subconscious, will direct us along the path to its fulfillment."** American Writer and Lecturer Joseph Campbell said, **"When you follow your bliss...doors will open where you would not have thought there would be doors; and where there wouldn't be a door for anyone else."**

You can learn about effective and efficient routes to your goals by learning from others who have gone before you and have accomplished similar goals. Learning from others, through conversation, books, workshops, presentations, etc. will help you confidently create your treasure map, which will guide you as you maneuver through the vast seas in all different areas of your life. Asking for advice and truly listening can be incredibly helpful as you put together your map. A Jewish Proverb states, **"No one is as deaf as the man who will not listen."** Former First Lady Eleanor Roosevelt said, **"Learn from the mistakes of others. You can't live long enough to make them all**

yourself." It will take hard work and lots of research as you put together your treasure map. Your determination and desire will be tested, as the path will not always be easily discovered.

However, as you passionately pursue your goals with your eyes and ears open, the map will become clearer. One tip is to recognize that the signs are everywhere helping to direct your life towards your goals and your purpose. Brazilian novelist Paulo Coelho said, **"We have this language of the omens, the language of the signs. It is an alphabet that is directed to us."** Pay attention to these signs. Renowned writer and philosopher Krishnamurti said, **"The moment you are very clear about what you want to do, things happen. Life comes to your aid."** When life comes to your aid, be present and open enough to recognize it and enjoy this assistance on your journey.

Do you know what your goals are? What do you need to do to reach your goals? What research could you do and who could help guide you towards more effective and/or efficient paths to achieving your goals? Are you paying attention to the signs?

CLIMB ABOARD

Are you ready, Captain? Today is the day to take your first step. You can start living your I-deal life today and be on your way to your ideal life. It's like English novelist George Eliot said, **"It's never too late to be what you might have been."** Write down today's date because today marks the day that everything began to change for you.

So climb aboard and begin your journey. Carpe Diem. Seize the day. German writer Johann Wolfgang von Goethe said, **"Whatever you can do, or dream you can, begin it. Boldness has genius, magic, and power in it."** You don't have to make all the changes in your life at once but you do need to make at least one. German scientist Georg C. Lichtenberg said, **"I cannot say whether things will get better if we change; what I can say is they must change if they are to get better."**

So review this booklet to determine areas in your life you feel you are in-need of some change. American author and speaker Price Pritchett said, **"Change always comes bearing gifts."** One small change can have a much bigger impact on your life than you may think. Sometimes you can't see the next big opportunity from your current position but it will be revealed to you once you take that first step. American civil rights leader Martin Luther King,

Jr. said, **"Faith is taking the first step even when you don't see the whole staircase."**

Are you ready to enhance your life? Former United States President Abraham Lincoln said, **"It's not the years in your life that count, it's the life in your years."** If you could use a little more 'life in your years', perhaps it's officially time to S.A.I.L. If you are ready to talk the talk and walk the walk, climb aboard! Living a life of integrity where your actions, words, and beliefs are all in-line with each other is a big part of living your ideal life. Indian spiritual and political leader Mahatma Gandhi said, **"Happiness is when what you think, what you say, and what you do are in harmony."**

So do as American author Mark Twain said, **"Twenty years from now you will be more disappointed by the things that you didn't do than by the ones you did. So throw off the bowlines. Sail away from the safe harbor. Catch the trade winds in your sails. Explore. Dream. Discover."** It's time for you to Select An Ideal Life!

What one change in your life will you begin working on right now? What sections of this booklet most clearly spoke to you and why? What are your next steps?

_____

_____

_____

_____

_____

_____

_____

_____

_____

_____

_____

_____

Select An Ideal Life - "Captain's Vows"

❏ I commit to fulfill my duty to be deeply happy

❏ I commit not to rush through life and to appreciate the unique journey of my life

❏ I commit to dreaming big and having a positive and proactive mindset

❏ I commit to taking full responsibility for my life

❏ I commit to not being afraid to make mistakes and to finding the lessons in all my missteps

❏ I commit to getting in touch with my inner-wisdom and trusting my instinct

❏ I commit to keeping a daily gratitude journal

❏ I commit to taking good care of my health

❏ I commit to developing positive relationships with supportive people and to supporting others to the best of my ability

❏ I commit to consistently developing my life-skills and using my greatest talents frequently

❏ I commit to regularly putting energy towards something bigger than myself

❏ I commit to seeking inspiration often and to looking around and noticing inspiring people and inspiring acts; big and small

❏ I commit to setting and seeking goals that reflect my passions and my definition of living successfully

❏ I commit to trusting that the route to my goals will unfold by passionately pursuing them, doing research and listening to the wisdom of others, and paying attention to the signs

❏ I commit to regularly assessing and re-assessing where I need to make improvements in my life and to taking one step forward today